DON´T LIE TO ME
Learn how to spot lies, understand body language and avoid manipulation

BY BASIL FOSTER AND JOSHUA MOORE

By Basil Foster and Joshua Moore

FREE DOWNLOAD

INSIGHTFUL GROWTH STRATEGIES FOR YOUR PERSONAL AND PROFESSIONAL SUCCESS!

Sign up here to get a free copy of The Growth Mindset book and more:
www.frenchnumber.net/growth

TABLE OF CONTENTS

Introduction 5
Chapter One: How Does Analyzing People Work Anyway? 8
    How to Start 10

Chapter Two: Personality Types 15
    The Personality Types 15
    The Spectrums in Lies 20
    The Most Likely Culprit – Identifying a Manipulator Type 25
    The Prey 28

Chapter Three: Reading Body Language 31
    Primitive Movements 33
    Evolving 37
    Putting in the Practice 39
    Key Gestures: 42

Chapter Four: Straight Up Lies 45
    What Actually Happens When Someone Lies? 46
    Lying Gestures 50
    False Positives – the Better Liars 51
    What Books Teach About How to Lie 54
    Quick Recap: 57

Chapter Five: The Facial Cues 59
    Cues: 59
        Fight, flight or freeze. 59
        Pacifiers. 60
    Micro-expressions 63
    Practice 66
    Recaps 67

Chapter Six: How Words Shape Reality 69
    Diction and Syntax 69
    Practice 73

   How Requests are Made.......................... 74

Chapter Seven: Analyzing Matters of the Heart/Home 79
   Lying and Cheating 80
   Matters of the Home................................... 83
   Confrontation 83
   Gaslighting... 85

Chapter Eight: Catching the Tiger by the Tail 88
   What Do the Professionals Do? 88
   Try It... 92
   Here is Some Practice:............................... 93

Introduction

It's not always easy to tell if a person is lying or trying to manipulate you. As much as we would love to be able to walk around and accept everything people tell us at face value, we can't. Ironically though, we're going to give a whole new meaning to face value because the face is a prime place to start observing if you want to discover those pesky, hidden intentions. Even the most inconspicuous reactions can give a person away completely. Have you ever noticed someone squint their eyes when they see you? If you found out later that they didn't like you, the eye squint was an overlooked sign. People tend to block things from their view that they are displeased with. Another common form of blocking things from view is by using the hand as a shield, this can be done by rubbing the brow or even by closing the eyes. While these actions are simple enough to read, you can think of them as tools in your arsenal of investigation.

If you want to find out if someone is lying to you, simply bring up what you suspect they are lying about. Think like an interrogator, ease your way in, start with the broad topic and slowly make your way to the specifics. Ask questions, and do most of the talking. If your suspect shows discomfort or exhibits one of the eye-blocking techniques, it's likely they don't like that you're onto them. However, context is of the utmost importance when trying to figure out someone's intentions. If you brazenly ask questions and monitor reactions without considering the context of the situation, you can misread the person you're trying to figure out.

You're not always stuck being the interrogator though, as you learn how to observe a person, you'll start to pick up on the tells as they talk to you. You'll notice if she rubs her collarbone, or if he pulls on the collar of his shirt. You may even notice the momentary flick of the hand in front of the mouth, signaling that person's discomfort with the words they are speaking. These observations come in time; to be able to read a person's intentions requires astute perception, a skill that will be honed through this practical guide.

You'll want to start with the basics. If you haven't spent a lot of time observing people, this would be a good time to start as you'll read about in the next chapter. But as a hint, you'll want to learn how to monitor people you're not interacting with, and people that you are. The latter is easier to stare at without too much suspicion. However, the easier it is for you to monitor someone you're not talking to, the easier it will be to judge a person's intentions before you even speak with them. This is a critical skill in some situations. We'll give you a quick example before we dive right in, if you're at a bar and a somewhat sober man approaches you with flaring nostrils, it would be a safe guess that you should prepare for a fight. If his nostrils are flaring but his stare is not dead set on you, he may just be mistaking you for a person he can vent to. However, we'll dive in to these a little more later on.

By Basil Foster and Joshua Moore

Chapter One: How Does Analyzing People Work Anyway?

In this day and age, we're not relying on voodoo or magic to determine whether or not a colleague is trying to make a subtle move to get that promotion or if that flirtatious woman over that at the corner of the bar just wants to steal your wallet. No, we're using cold, hard science and proven methods to profile potential suspects and size up the competition. By enhancing our naturally occurring intuition with scientific facts and federally proven and trusted psychological methods for detecting deceit, we're simply armoring ourselves with a bullet proof vest for all those people walking around with ammo built from lies. There is no reason to let those deceit shaped bullets pierce our chests and destroy our trust. We need to focus on defense instead of learning how to cope after the damage is done.

As social beings we rely on interactions with others as an integral part of our survival. We have to be respectful to our bosses, authoritative to our children and somewhere in-between for everyone else. But some people take this dependence on interaction a step further and use such it to get what they want and need out of others. To protect yourself and the ones you love, you need to be able to turn the very same fundamentals against them, using psychology.

Salesmen use psychology to better move products, marketers use it to influence people's attention, interrogators use psychology to understand what their suspect is lying about or thinking. Counselors use psychology to understand what is disturbing or causing discomfort in their client's life. Time and time again, psychology is being used to understand what people do and how they do it.

Since a way to peek into a person's mind already exists, all we have to do is to tap into that flow of information! When people lie, there are tells. They're aptly named because subtle clues, a head nod, a shifted gaze, a comforting gesture, are all ways of telling you, you're being deceived.

While there are several sure-fire methods to uncovering the truth behind a person's actions, we're going to focus on the most effective and least time consuming so that you may integrate our methods into your everyday life seamlessly. From psychological profiling to analyzing facial cues, body language and diction, we've got you covered. This book will be your practical guide to learning how to analyze people in no time at all and it'll be a breeze.

We know that simply providing a book on only one of methods for lie detection would be like giving you a pizza cutter and a slice of a pizza, that's practically useless! The pizza has already been cut, there would be practically no point in it.

By Basil Foster and Joshua Moore

You'd want a full pizza if you had the pizza cutter. Learning to use all of the methods available to you together, will give you a thorough understanding of the ins and outs of manipulation. So, we'll give you the full pizza and the pizza cutter and you can cut it up however you want.

How to Start

Now, just reading about it won't make you an adept analyzer, so, let's get to the nitty gritty already. Our next topic covers personality types and typically, you won't know much about a person's personality unless you've spent some time with them. You may be able to tell me that Joe, the friend you've had for five years is a go-getter who doesn't take no for an answer, he's honest to a fault, but doesn't take criticism well, but would you be able to tell me anything about the new employee who started three days ago? Probably not. Limited interaction doesn't always leave the seemingly large amount of time needed to get to know someone. Sure, you could just say that the new employee looks nice, but does that really tell you what kind of person she is? While it isn't uncommon to just take people at face value and what they look like, we know better than that. The days without inspection are over, from now on we read into the tells people exhibit while they talk. So, put on your detective cap, because everything is going to be an open case from here on out.

Observation is Key
If you want to cultivate the ability to read people, you're going to have to start observing those around you more often. After all, you wouldn't be able to read words on a page if you couldn't discriminate between the letters on that page! So, we've thrown together a little guide on how you can start training yourself to be a bit more observational, that way you'll be able to discriminate the letters of the deception alphabet a little better.

Since it may be a little difficult at first, set up intervals of time throughout your day where you can sit and watch others. Coffee shops, parks, or bars are all common places for people to convene. Even if you only have 30 minutes on your lunch break, watch how people at your workplace interact with each other, you don't have to solely focus on them, you can eat your sandwich while you watch.

Start by seeing how people react to each other, without involving yourself. Here are a few basics to observe: the mood of the conversation, the flow of the conversation, and what can you tell from the body language on display. You don't need to know what every gesture means, but you may already have a basic understanding of common signs. For instance, if someone has an angry face and is viciously pointing their finger at the other person, you can conclude they are angry at that person for something they did. If

they are pointing their finger in another direction, you could say they are angry at something or someone else.
Whether you take time from your lunch break or set a reminder on your phone for random points in the day, try to spend a little more time observing – this will be an imperative skill for the later chapters. The more you're used to watching people and analyzing what they are doing the easier it will be able to pick up on tells we'll teach you.

Conversation with Intent
Once you've spent a couple days just observing people and how they interact, try to hold a conversation with intent. To be able to read people during a conversation, you have to be able to intently observe without losing track of your conversation, or coming off as suspicious or weird to the other person. A good start may be by trying to find a friend and a topic you can discuss with them. The topic could really be about anything, as the matter of conversation is unimportant. While holding your conversation try to pay attention to how they act and react while they are talking. Was that head-nod a physical representation of the direction they were just referring to and did they inadvertently shrug their shoulders when referring to a topic they knew nothing about?
These seemingly insignificant tells could be the sole reason you realize someone is lying to you. If you've picked up on the fact someone will nod

their head in a direction they're talking about and all of a sudden, they say they went left but their head moves to motion towards the right, you've caught the bull by the horns. No tell is insignificant.

During this exercise you can try to hold conversations of intent with as many different subjects as you'd like. You don't have to focus on learning one person.

Try to connect the dots between gestures and words or phrases. It's okay if you're not sure about what they all mean, but the longer you observe these ticks, the more you'll be able to pick up on them when we get to the more in-depth chapters on facial expressions, body language and diction. Once you've spent a comfortable amount of time connecting the dots between gestures and what people are talking about, try to consider their facial expressions too. During your conversations, when your subject talks about something that excites them, do their eyes light up, do the crow's feet show? Does their lip quiver during a topic that upsets them? Every action and reaction has a meaning, some may be irrelevant and some may directly correlate with the topic you are talking about – it's important to be able to differentiate, and we're starting that learning process now.

Remember, you are just observing and seeing what you already know and what already stands out to you. You don't have to skip ahead and find out what certain ticks mean, we will cover all of that in due time.

By Basil Foster and Joshua Moore

Once you've gotten the hang of the exercises above, you'll be more than ready to move onto the next chapter.

Chapter Two: Personality Types

Knowing someone's personality is a great tool to have in your utility belt if people that are close to you are lying to you, but what about someone you've just met? Are you just supposed to let them lie to you and manipulate you while you learn their personality type? No. But, it's especially important to know if a person is just quirky by nature or if quirkiness is because of the cognitive dissonance of deceit. So, learning to pick up on a personality type quickly is key.

You may have heard of these theories before, if you were taking personality quizzes online, or whether you heard them in school, they have been pretty prevalent.

The Personality Types

Personalities bring out motivational factors that may not be present in regular situations. But if you know that Joe is an extrovert who feels deeply, you may realize that the reason he lied last Tuesday was because he weighs the importance of his social circle and didn't want to disappoint his friends. Motivation is key to any police investigation, and it'll be a key in yours too. You can't put together a full puzzle if you're missing a piece. Personality is a piece.

First, we'll talk about the Myers and Briggs Type Indicator or MBTI for short.

The MBTI is referred to as a personality inventory, there are four different categories with two different possibilities. It may help you to look at it as though in each category there is a spectrum. A person can fall anywhere between the two. This provides sixteen different possibilities, but you don't have to bother learning them, it's not important for what we're trying to accomplish. Below, we've outlined the different spectrums, and how you can tell who will fall into what category. This will be important for determining what kind of person you're going to be analyzing.

- **Extroverts   -   Introverts**: Quite bluntly, those who are energized and enjoy socializing with others, are going to be the extroverts of this category. While in contrast, those who prefer to energize in isolation and are more reserved are the introverts.
- **Thinkers   -   Feelers** Thinkers rely on rationalizations to navigate their world and often weigh the pros and the cons of situations. Thinkers may offer advice based on what way would be most rational choice, rather than how it would affect emotions. Feelers conversely, would rather let their heart lead. They would prefer to make a

decision based on which option may feel right, and may weight how their choices would affect effect the feelings of others.
- **Sensors – Intuitives**: Sensors may use numbers and statistics or rely on prior experience to make decisions. They prefer practical solutions derived from their sense of the world. Intuitives often look at the bigger picture of their issues. They may weigh the possibilities, or patterns, and they seek creative solutions instead of what may sensible and practical to others.
- **Judgers – Perceivers**: Judgers are those who like to be organized and prepared. Information, routines, and plans are their friends. Judgers may be a stickler for rules. Perceivers like to watch things unfold, they may be quiet in their observations. They gather information like spies.

If you like to remember phrases, you may want to try these two: "Even the Sires Jest" the first letter of each word correlates to Extroverts, Thinkers, Sensors and Judgers. The other half may be remembered with the phrase, "Important Friends Improve Performance" meaning: Introverts, Feelers, Inuitives, and Perceivers.

Or if you prefer to remember acronyms try: JEST – Judgers, Extroverts, Sensors and Thinkers. The second half can be remembered by PIIF – Perceivers, Introverts, Intuitives, and Feelers.

Once you remembered the acronym, it's rather easy figure out how to categorize a person. You may have noticed that you can easily assimilate these categories together to create stereotypical personality types, it's true. An introvert is likely to be a perceiver, and by being a perceiver prefers the bigger picture, making them an intuitive as well, and lastly, you can easily see if they make decisions based on emotions or pros and cons.

If you're looking to efficiently identify a person's personality type, try using some of these to pick up on their personality. Don't be afraid to sit back and observe when you have the chance. You don't have to be an active part of the conversation to learn more about someone. Since you can already remember the categories and their names, if you're having trouble remembering what aspects fit what category use the below guide:

- Think of Judgers as Judges: they like an organized and planned proceedings of court affairs. They rely on gathering information from defendants or prosecutors to decide. Judges always enforce the rules.
- Perceivers are going to perceive or observe things from different points of views, and through their observations

piece together the needed information.

- Sensors are literally sensors. Sensors on cars gather statistics and data, this type of information allows them to sense whether or not a car is beside them (sensors on vehicles), or if motion has been made (motion detectors). A sensor could never extrapolate information out of its field. For example, motion detectors only know if something has moved, not if something has moved while the door is open or closed.
- Intuitives are intuition. Intuition is the ability to know something without reasoning. If you have a gut feeling (intuition) you know that someone is lying without knowing the details as to why, thus you already know the bigger picture (they've lied) and not the smaller details (the behaviors that told you why they lied). They often weigh possibilities from patterns (you got the gut feeling from their behavior pattern).

- Thinkers are all about thinking logically. Thoughts are often rationalized, and by doing so require weighing the good and the bad, or the possibility versus

impossibility. Logic is all about getting from point a to point b because of c.
- Feelers rely on feelings. How they feel, how others feel, and how they would feel or how others would feel based on possible outcomes.

- Extroverts are extra, they want to socialize, be around others and be full and complete and overflowing.
- Introverts are all about inter, whether it's their own feelings or emotions, or isolation and reservation, all of that spurns from solitude.

Now that's we've reviewed how to identify these personality types, here are a few outlines of why someone in these categories may want to pick a bone of deceit, and in some cases, what they may lie about.

The Spectrums in Lies

First and foremost, we'll start with Extroverts.
Extroverts versus Introverts
- Extroverts, who value their reputation and appearances amongst crowds, may have illusions of grandeur. These illusions may make them prone to embellishing

what they have accomplished or what they've read, heard or saw. It may also fuel their desire to lie. If anything starts to threaten their reputation there is no telling what they may say or do to try to keep what they value so dearly in check.

- There is always the grandeur factor. If getting away with a lie or manipulation may prove their dominance and is accepted by their crowd or even encouraged there is no telling how far they will go to prove their mightiness.
- Some extroverts will get a secret thrill out of what they can get away with. They may go to a club and pretend to be someone they aren't. Maybe it's a rich sophisticated individual or someone of the more devious nature (bad boy/girl) that will get attention. They are motivated to manipulate to fulfill attention-related desires

- Introverts may lie to defend their close relationships or their isolation. If pretending that they are sick or that they don't get along with others can get them time to themselves, you bet they're on board.

- To keep to themselves, they may often feign reasons to not go to populated outings.
- An introvert who may feel cornered could manipulate or lie to maintain a relationship they feel is on the fence.

Feelers versus Thinkers
- Feelers may fear letting others down or may fear eliciting disappointment in others, this fear may motivate them to weave webs of deceit in order to remain in good standing with others.
- The emotions of others, if for some reason they feel that someone may not be able to handle information or that certain things may upset someone, they could go completely out of their way to lie through so that person doesn't have to become upset. Feelers are prone to sparing feelings at the cost of their honesty.
- Some feelers may believe that because they are empathetic they always have to do what is best for the majority and may weigh lying for the greater good as a necessary evil.
- Some may let their devious hearts lead, even if it's down a path of deceit, just for the simple thrill of it!

DON´T LIE TO ME

- Thinkers may judge a situation based on the pros and cons of lying or not lying. If they think that there is more to gain from their deception then they think there is no reason not to lie.
- Thinkers can get caught up in the rationales, if it seems more rational to them to lie rather than tell the truth, they are not going to waste their time with the truth. If the lie is the logical conclusion, they're going to take it.

Judgers and Perceivers

- Judgers may feel like they know all of the possibilities to a lie's end because they may have planned thoroughly ahead to make sure they expound each detail and avenue of possibility perfectly.
- Judgers can get a high and mighty approach to lying. They may be more prone to become chronic liars as they have planned, prepared and thought through the lies. If they think they are smart enough to continuous get away with deceit, they just might.
- Some Judgers may lie and manipulate as their own way of upholding the rules and laws that they feel should govern the world like lines of black and white.

- Perceivers, in their usually laid-back manner may lie, if they feel threatened, in order to uphold their perceiving nature, lies may be the cost they are willing to pay.
- Having spent a majority of their time observing, the may be lured into a false sense of security. Once they realize their security has been breached, they may lie to gain that security back.
- Perceivers, who have spent most of their time learning and acquiring information on society, may lie to uphold societal norms, or manipulate those who don't already conform into conforming to the norms that should be upheld.

Sensors and Intuitives
- Sensors who have successfully lied in the past are more likely to lie about the same things in the future. If pushed to lie about something they haven't tried before they may seek comfort in the possibility of their lie being believed.
- If a sensor has sense of the world dependent upon deceit, possibly from learned behaviors, they may feel like the world would not make sense without lies.

- Intuitives, having thought of a creative solution to a problem, may use lies as a

way to expand their horizons and creativity. They are most likely to spin webs of brilliant lies, and may even expound too far into the details.
- Since honesty may be a practical solution to a problem, they may choose manipulation as a fun outlandish way arrive at a conclusion.

The Most Likely Culprit – Identifying a Manipulator Type

As you'll learn about later on in the book, body language is a great way to tell if someone is saying, or thinking something that may be disturbing or discomforting, but some people have natural tendencies to do certain actions. Like those with Asperger's or any form of autism, often display comforting mannerisms because that is their natural pacifier for their state; not because they are trying to deceive anyone. But there are those whose sole purpose is to deceive, and they will do all that they can to convince you of their lies.

While a manipulator may be of any personality type and may be trying to get their way for any innumerable reasons, there are common traits of a manipulator that you can look out for, and thanks to the Health Psychology Consultancy, we know what those traits are. We can use these exhibited traits as huge red flags that should be made note of and added to your arsenal if knowledge. While some people are just regular individuals who may be uncomfortable manipulating you to get what they want, there are others who set out to manipulate as their sole goal. It's important to be able to identify these individuals as well as the other average joes who just want to tell you a lie so you look the other way.

Some of the common characteristics of a manipulator according to Health Psychology Consultancy, are:

Deceitful, compelling, controlling, self-conscious, and paranoid. These are the key traits of a person you want to avoid and thankfully at the end of this book you'll be able to identify deceit with ease. Those who want to be controlling or compelling may be easy to spot thanks to their impeding presence. Controlling behaviors can only be masked for so long. Self-conscious individuals can be spotted due to their instinctual recoils, and those who are paranoid are high anxiety and you'll learn plenty of anxiety related tells later on.

Because these individuals are so complex and eager to manipulate, they will seek out certain prey that would be easy bait. Manipulators don't care if they break societal rules or hurt people's feelings, they will use whatever means necessary to get to whatever end they desire. Manipulators can be hard to spot with their constantly moving pieces, they try to cover their tails so thoroughly it could be like trying to pin the tail on the donkey. Typically, those trying to identify a manipulator have a nagging suspicion that gets shrugged off for a lack of verifiable evidence. Or because they've employed tactics to pull sympathy from their victims. But no more, shall you even let the possibility of a manipulator ruin or rule you. You will be armed to the T with the information to spot a skirt a manipulator.

Sociopaths
Manipulators could be further categorized into a sociopath. Sociopaths have always been scary individuals for their tremendous talent and ability, their obvious lack of remorse and the over abounding charm make them a worthy foe of the people analyzer. You may further identify them by their unreliability, their insincerity or their inability to have a person sexual life or personal life. Because sociopaths are incapable of love, they are often isolated and superficial, but they may have a narcissistic view of themselves.
Sociopaths are ones that would lie and manipulate just because they feel superior to others. It could provide them will a thrill that they could hardly elicit from any other situation. While sociopaths may seem like a great villain for a TV show and nothing else, they aren't fairy tales made to scare individuals. They do coexist and being able to identify one could easily save you a lot of hurt.

By Basil Foster and Joshua Moore

The Prey

These manipulator types like to seek out specific victims, people who are easy for them to manipulate as a way to stimulate their bloodlust. If someone puts up too much of a fight, the manipulator may no longer want to contrive their schemes especially if they think they may lose. However, sometimes individuals who are heartier and more difficult to manipulate are just seen a personal challenge for this kind of individual – especially if they are trying to advance their skill.

So, who do manipulators seek out the most?

Simple: those who are meek, seem like they are people pleasures, and those who yearn for approval and acceptance. Commonly, those who seem to lack the ability to say no (quite typically these also fall into the people pleaser category), and those who to have low self-confidence are also chosen as prey for the manipulator type. Lastly, those who seem naïve and ready to give anyone, even the manipulator the benefit of the doubt are also easy pickings.

Quite obviously, those who seem easy to manipulate are the ones the manipulator goes after the most. These specific prey types are easy to persuade with words of fame, glory or fortune, or promises of acceptance and the façade of benevolence. If a person seeks approval, they don't want to elicit disapproval or negative emotions from the manipulator, so they will bend over backwards for that approval. This is exactly what the manipulator or sociopath would feed on.

For those fretting they fall into that category: If you don't want to be seen as easy prey, try to work on your outward presentation. Don't slouch (it resembles the turtle stance of trying to hide so you go unnoticed and is seen as a sign of weakness), look people straight in their eyes (not for too long), and don't be afraid to say no. Practice saying no. Practice appearing confident. Even just appearing to be more confident and steadfast than you really are can at least ward off those who don't pry too much.

If the manipulator is close enough to you though, they will be able to see your weaknesses through the façade. If you can spot the manipulator first, you will know who to put your foot down to – but if you don't practice how you play, there is no real way to know that you will definitely not allow the manipulator to manipulate you. You could fall into the pit of, "I know they're a manipulator, but maybe..." and that will lead to a desert of despair.

The only way to fully ward off manipulators is to work on being less of each of those easy prey aspects. You have to say no in all areas of your life. To be more confident, to accept yourself as you are – without needing approval from another, and learn that not everyone can always have the benefit of the doubt. Giving that little leeway is like giving someone an and inch and not expecting them to take the mile. They will take the mile.

By Basil Foster and Joshua Moore

Chapter Three: Reading Body Language

Body language is a universal language, while inevitably there are some regional nuances, for the most part, you'll be able to appraise a person and read into their thoughts solely from the displays of their body. We've already started exercises in chapter one on observing people, so by now, you should be pretty comfortable observing a person both in conversation and out.

We're going to break down some of the common, more applicable aspects of reading body language so that you're not bogged down with excessive, possibly useless information.

Context is key. A person will react to numerous stimuli in their vicinity. You have to be aware of the changes in the environment or just the status of the environment to know if your subject is reacting to you or an increased room temperature. As the detector, you have to keep track of the changes in the environment. You need to know if a light is flickering, it will be a distraction. You have to notice if the air has kicked in and it's getting colder in the room. Are there annoying sounds? Displeasing aesthetics? Anything and everything is important.

Importance of the Environment

So, the very first exercise in learning body language is to notice the things going on around you. Start up a conversation with a person you're intent on observing and make sure you notice without missing parts of the conversation what is going on. Take a mental note if something changes so you can monitor the new baseline of behavior. If for instance, the air conditioner does kick on in the middle of your conversation with someone, take note of when it turns off again. Wait a few moments for things to baseline again, and then bring up the pervious parts of the conversation the person reacted to. If they rubbed their arms while they spoke, they may have been cold, but if they do it again and the temperature has started to warm up, it could be a sign of unease.

Learning a Baseline

Any successful interrogator knows to establish a baseline with their suspect before they move towards taboo subjects that may cause discomfort. Once a baseline is established all future gesticulations and motions can be compared to a truthful, foundational display.

Previously, we've learned about and practiced identifying personality types, and doing it quickly. For this section, finding a personality type and identifying their baseline behavior is key. Baseline behavior and personality go hand in hand.

You may not fully be aware of the baseline behavior of even people that are close to you. So, take some time to start conversations with individuals and establish their personality and baseline. Take the conversation to multiple topics. Start with very neutral subjects, move to more passion invoking ones and happier ones back to neutral.

Once you've spent some time getting accustomed to changes in the environment and establishing a baseline, you're ready to start learning what the gestures you've been noticing mean.

Primitive Movements

There are different kinds of body language. Most actions are conscious, meaning they can be faked or omitted at will. True liars versed in the ways of deceit know this and use this to their advantage. Everyday citizens who may only lie on occasion to save face, may not be as well versed. That is where our advantage lies. We want to be able to distinguish our usually loving co-workers sudden interest in our project as a power play. Thankfully though, there are primitive reactions that happen subconsciously and are far more reliable some of the gesticulations that can be faked. For the sake of diversity, we'll cover both.

Freeze, flight or fight? More often than not, a person will freeze to evaluate whether or not fight or flight is the appropriate reaction to their situation. It could be a split-second freeze, that happens just long enough for the perpetrator to send a signal to their brain to unfreeze. Look for the freeze.

By Basil Foster and Joshua Moore

Have you ever caught a child sneaking into the proverbial, metaphorical cookie jar? If they even start to hear someone's footsteps they may freeze before they react in any other way. If you've caught them and you speak to announce your presence, they are sure to pause and they'll probably even turn around slowly to discover your presence.

Just as a child will pause when caught, a manipulator will pause. An average person lying may not think anything of their sudden freezing movement, but a full-fledged manipulator may only let the freeze last a split-second, may play the freeze off as a different reaction, or even try to convince you there was a freeze at all.

People don't just freeze for a physical threat, they freeze at thoughts. Have you ever paused suddenly in the middle of an action because you remembered something? The same will happen to a manipulator if they think they've been caught or if they think they are in danger of being discovered.

A form of flight. Often times, when people are feeling threatened in some way, they will find ways to put distance between them and the negative stimuli or they will find a barrier. Distance can be achieved by simply taking a step back, leaning back or completely existing the room/situation. If while standing, you notice a person leaning back away from you, they may be starting to feel threatened.

Continuing with the child metaphor, have you

ever watched a child try to hide or sneak? What do they do? They either cover their eyes, thinking that if they can't see you, you can't see them, or they try to make themselves smaller. If they hunch over and walk passed you, suddenly they are camouflaged and you can't see them – or so they hope. You can watch a child who has done something wrong try to exit the room hunched over. The same is true for adults who are trying to get away with lying, however, with time to grow up, adults tend to change how they hunch over.

While, an adult in trouble is just as likely to try to become a turtle: pull their shoulders up and forward and tuck their head down as the try to gaze towards the floor, there are also other displays of trying to hide.

Barriers. Other times, simple barriers will do. Have you ever noticed someone put their ankle on their knee, forming a table on their lap? The shin facing outward is a barrier. It's a form of keeping threats at bay. So, if you're having a sitting conversation with someone and you notice they start to lean back in their chair and prop their leg up to form a barrier between you and them, you may want to take note of the topic. While this may be a sign they just don't agree with your view, it could also be worth exploring the topic a little more, especially if you've already got the sense that something is off.

Some people may pick up objects to act as a barrier between you and them instead of changing their body position. The same way children have security blankets or stuffed animal they can press against their chest, lying adults may also want a security blanket of sorts. Pillows on couches are often grabbed, if there are no items, the arms could be placed across the chest.

Check the Feet. Just as looking at the bottom of someone's feet will tell you where they've been, looking at the direction of the feet will tell you where they are going. While this phrase may seem obvious, looking at the direction someone's feet is pointing will tell you where they *want* to be. If a person is sitting on a couch, but have moved their feet to face the door, they may be ready to leave. This becomes especially true if they've moved their stance to prepare for standing up, like scooting towards the edge of the cushion and leaning forward, ready to shift their weight to their legs.

People can point their feet in the direction they want to go if they are uncomfortable and they want to leave the current situation faster. Just like leaving the scene of a crime before the law enforcement shows up. While not everyone is going to want to flee the conversation because you've brought up something they may be lying about, some will especially if they can use leaving as an excuse to not have to talk about it. Leaving gives them more time to think of what to say, how to say it and how to come off as truthful or convince you it was all a misunderstanding.

Locking. Women are more prone to locking their legs or ankles because they've been taught to sit this way, especially when wearing a skirt. However, if a man interlocks his ankles while sitting he is displaying a high level of stress and it should raise a red flag. For either gender, sudden locking of the ankles is a sign that something may be off. Prolonged ankle locking is a way of restricting movement.

Just as the freeze instinct suggestions, people tend to cease their movements when they are lying. If someone has been using gestures frequently and suddenly ceases, this may be an indication that they have started lying. If someone's feet have been moving regularly during a conversation, especially while sitting and they suddenly cease, take note.

Evolving

Joe Navarro an FBI agent trained in interrogation states that after every primitive response, there will be a pacifying behavior. These behaviors are mechanisms to calm anxiety or fear. They are big discomfort flags.

Going for the Neck. The neck is the most prominent pacifying area. Men like to rub their necks, touch their collars or pull on their ties, women will play with necklaces, or touch around their collar bone and center of the neck.

Sometimes, when a woman puts her arms across

her chest, she is actually cupping her right elbow with her left hand. When she does this she is putting a barrier between her and the person she is talking to. If things get really uncomfortable, she will move her right hand to her neck. She may play with a necklace or touch her fingers to her neck to display her discomfort.

The Cleanser. The cleanser is a well-known sign of discomfort or stress. Have you ever noticed someone rubbing their hands, or more accurately, their palms down their thighs? This action can be done once or repetitiously depending on why the reaction is occurring. The cleanser could be used for two reasons, the person has started to sweat (possibly from anxiety), or because the person is using it to pacify. With either reasoning the cleanser is a behavior to notice. The subject may be more prone to use it if they think a table is blocking the view of their thighs and palms. An easy way to still notice the cleanser is to watch the elbows/arms and shoulders if their hands have disappeared under the table, you will still see a forward and backwards motion in these regions.

All kinds of primitive or pacifying behavior can be used as a clue that something more than meets the eye is going on. It's usually these kinds of reactions that our subconscious picks up on to tell us that something fishy is happening anyway. So, once you have the clues that you need from actively paying attention to what strikes the nerve in your subject, you'll know what topics to peruse. If as you speak about the questionable topic, and more uncomfortable body language is displayed, you can ask questions. Asking seemingly genuine questions is a great way to get them talking and to analyze their reactions to what they are saying. If they display any of the body language discussed in the next chapter, you may want to consider the possibility you're being lied to or manipulated.

Keep in mind the real meaning of these gesticulations though, they aren't gestures of liars rather people who have been made uncomfortable or are stressed for some reason. People can become uncomfortable or stressed for many more reasons than just deceit. Don't jump to conclusions until, like a covert spy you've gathered all the intel you need to make your case.

Putting in the Practice

Now that we've discussed the demonstrations of discomfort, it's time to employ the information you've uncovered. After all, utilizing knowledge you've acquired aids the retention process. Spend some time in your usual conversation allocation to try to identify things that people react to in the ways we've discussed. If you'd like to start pointing out discrepancies in people's words without being too conspicuous, then try asking questions on something that seems off to you. Practice gleaning information without straight confrontation. Try to monitor the person's reaction. Discern if they are just caught off guard, nervous or attempting to deceive? You may not know the answer to that question yet, but start picking up on the freeze, flight or fight responses.

Don't confront the person about it afterwards, it's likely that without the use of other tells your results are skewed. Just as you can't tell what kind of pie a person has by the crust alone, you won't know completely whether or not the person is lying without more information. These practices are just to get you used to picking up on these displays, the crust of the pie, if you will. Spies don't run to their suspect with insubstantial evidence and neither should you. Or, if an interrogator went into a room trying to confront a suspect one a single discrepancy the whole case could blow up in their face. Neither result is as desired. So be patient and gather the information you need.

Now, let's put this to use in an example.

You've started a conversation with your friend, the two of you are talking about a party that you both attended last week. You mention to your friend it was rather disappointing that he had to head home before the afterparty started and at the emergence of the sentence he suddenly pauses in the middle of setting his drink down. It only lasts a second, he gives an awkward chuckle with an exhale, "yeah" is his response.

Immediately, he asks if you were able to catch the game the next day.

When you ask him what happened after he left the party, he rubs one hand down his thigh and leans back in his chair. After a short pause he leans forward again, "Well, man. I ran into one of the women from the party and we ended up going to a bar."

In the party of the conversation, his pause allows you to know that there's something more to what happened on his way home from the party. He switches the subject as a fleeing method to keep from having to continue on a discomforting topic. This leaves a few options:

1. He blew off the afterparty for something else.
2. Something interrupted his journey or plans to go home.
3. Something happened after he left the party that he didn't want you to know about or that was uncomfortable to him.

Th second half of the last option is very important because it could have been as simple as he remembered something unpleasant about that evening. He could have come home from the party only to realize he accidently grabbed another man's wallet or a close friend was upset and waiting for him at the doorstep. He could have even remembered how upset him leaving had made someone and had forgotten to apologize.

With body language, there is no secret key that

will tell you what is going on in the brain. You can only get glimpses into the mind that help you analyze the person and the situation. You have to be aware of the possibilities and how to get to the logical, possible conclusion instead of what you might want the conclusion to be.

Remember if you want to prove that someone is lying to you, you will prove someone is lying to you. Your mind will skew any bit of information into a biased set of details. It's even called coercion. You can make someone admit to lying to you even if they never did if you are aggressive enough about it. So, keep your analysis open-minded.

If you want to prove that someone is lying to you, first try to prove that they are not lying to you. With real genuine evidence. This will be a little easier later on when you know what tone of voice to look for, what words may be biased, and you have a more complete picture of what is going on. If you find

Key Gestures:

Here's a quick review of some of the things we've discussed in this chapter. The more important tidbits have been outlined below so you won't have to skim the entirety of the chapter to find something you may need to brush up on.

Freeze: Freezing can happen in any region of the body, or the whole body. Freezing allows time to

access the situation and appraise current knowledge.
- Check for active feet that suddenly stop. Or, gestures that suddenly cease or are reduced in number. Typically, in stressful situations, once the situation is determined no longer a threat the motions will resume.

Flee: Pointed feet display a person's desired direction. People often want to escape stressful situations, or buy more time for themselves if at all possible.

Leans: Leaning away is a non-active form of fleeing. It puts distance between the person and the source of their displeasure.

Barriers: Barriers are a way to keep things that we don't want near us away. Natural barriers include a propped leg, or crossed arms. Other objects may also be placed between the person and the source of their displeasure. Children may use blankets as a barrier, adults may grab a pillow and press it to their chest, or seemingly hide behind a purse.

Rubs: In this chapter we covered how a person may rub their ear as a way to 'block' the words they don't want to hear, or to pacify. The cleanser is another form of rubbing: the palms rub down the thighs as a way to pacify stress.

Lock: Locked legs or ankles, especially in men and for prolonged periods denotes the feeling of being threatened.

Neck: Both men and women tend to cover their neck when they are uncomfortable or are stressed. Women may touch the middle of their neck or around their neckbones. Men tend to play with their collars and/or rub the back or sides of their necks.

Chapter Four: Straight Up Lies

Oh, what a tangled web we we've when we learn to deceive. This saying could not be truer. If an individual is trying to pull the wool over your eyes, they are creating an intricately tangled web. Pulling at just one of these strings will uncover the stress of where the rest of the deceit lies.

During conversation a red flag is raised, something seems off about the person you're conversating with. It's likely that you've subconsciously picked up on some of the tells of a lie. Be observant, find out what exactly creates a response in your subject. Then, pull the string and see what unweaves.

Lies fail because of fear. From young children we are taught that punishment is something to fear, we don't want to be spanked, be put in time out or have our favorite toys taken away from us. As adults we may lose reputation, lose the trust of a friend, or get fired. These consequences fuel our desire to remain truthful, and fuel a liar's desire not to be caught. With such important aspects of our lives on the line, fear leaks in and causes nervous/uncomfortable or defensive gesticulations that give away our lies.

When bad liars think they are going to be caught in a lie they may dig their hole deeper, if they haven't had time to plan a deeper pit, it will be pretty easy to kick them into it. Liars under pressure they haven't prepared for will falter. Straight falsehoods are hard to keep up with, if everything a liar is saying is fabricated, there is a good chance they'll forget some aspects of their lie. An easy way to catch the tiger by the tail is to ask about it again. Feign ignorance on the subject and ask for an explanation. Pretend you didn't clearly hear what they have said, and ask them to repeat it.

The trick: experiences talked about are easier to remember. There should be almost no issues reiterating something that has happened or was already explained.

The pitfall: it's pretty common to hear that lies are better based on facts. A misleading truth is harder to identify than a lie. Misleads may be close enough to the truth that they're easier to remember. Since not all the details have been fabricated, there are less strings to pull to unweave the web of deceit. More successful liars will use this technique because if all else fails, they can play the lie off as a misunderstanding.

What Actually Happens When Someone Lies?

Lying typically causes cognitive dissonance within the liar, if they aren't addicted to lying that is. Cognitive dissonance is described as a conflict between emotions or beliefs and what is actually being done. This dissonance causes the sympathetic nervous system to activate and physiological signs to emerge, especially when coupled with the fear or anxiety of being caught. Some physiological cues are hardly noticeable, unless you're intimate with someone, but others may be a little more conspicuous.

While it may not be blatant, people often sweat when they lie due to the activation of the sympathetic nervous system. The person may also have a sudden shortness of breath. Both of these cues are more noticeable the closer you are to the individual. If there is adequate personal space, these minute changes may not be visible.
Other signs that may not be as noticeable, increased heart rate and increased blood pressure.
If you're speaking with a loved one, it may be easier to note the increased heart rate if you're touching their wrist, or somewhere where the pulse is strong, or your head is on their chest. You may also be able to pick up the sweat as their skin becomes moist. But for those you are not as intimate with, no worries these signs are only aids and are not necessary aids to discovering the veil of deceit.

For others, where proximity may be an issue the other signs to pick up on are listed below.
Eyes: Pupils may narrow during a lie, or

unconsciously flick from one direction to another. Some neuro-linguists believe that people look up and left to lie and up and right when telling the truth, but this is conditional and may change from person to person. To really test, try to find a baseline by asking questions that require memory and see which way the eyes go to normally. If a person just choses a side at random, you should rely on other tells to arm your intuition.

As a quick tidbit: as a person grows more nervous, they may blink more often than usual. People who aren't used to being recorded may blink at an increased rate when placed in front of a potentially recording camera. The same is true of those who may fear a person 'seeing right through them' and their lies.

Mouth/Throat: Sometimes manipulators try to smile through their lies, on the notion that the smile will disarm their prey. When you're uncertain if a smile is genuine or fake, look to the eyes. Typically, during faked smiles, the eyes don't relax the way they usually would. The cheeks bring the muscles around the eyes up, crow's feet form. Take some time to observe people when they are genuinely smiling, they've heard something that makes them happy or however, but make a mental note of how their faces contort. If you observe how the people you interact with commonly, smile you'll know when they fake it. If you observe enough people you will be able to see fake smiles a mile away.

Those who haven't been lying as long may find they have a hard swallow when they are lying or starting to lie. Other signs would be licking the lips consistently.

Nervousness: The nervous energy abounds with deceit. People who are excessively nervous may be found fidgeting. This fidgeting serves a two-fold purpose, it gives an outlet for the energy the builds with nervousness and it seems to be a useful distraction for an excuse. If someone seems distracted, it would be harder to decipher their gestures, and it would mask their gestures. For instance, they wouldn't be as inclined to pull on their collar or cover their neck if they've decided to tie their shoe.

Someone who finds distractions during the conversation may be trying to cover up gestures that would otherwise give them away. It may be useful to note the topic of conversation so you can visit it again at a later time, when distractions don't abound.

Be careful of nervous energy; there are plenty of reasons for a person to become nervous. Some individuals are more nervous than others, some have naturally high anxiety. These are all imperative aspects to check for before taking a sudden nervous tick as a sign of deceit.

Finally, defensive gestures, like displaying barriers, or displaying discomfort/stress will be more common.

By Basil Foster and Joshua Moore

Lying Gestures

Mouth Cover: A form of blocking, the most prominent gesture of a bad liar is covering the mouth. If a person doesn't like the words they are speaking, doesn't agree with them, or doesn't believe them, they may cover their mouth while they speak. This can be a full mouth cover, a partial mouth cover, or even a single finger. If the hand is on or near to the mouth, even touching it slightly, it may be a subconscious ploy to block the lying words. The subtle version of this gesture is rubbing the bottom of the nose, or the liar may start to bring their hand to their mouth but reroute it. This may result in a hand being brought up, paused and then redirected.

Beware though, a person may have an itchy nose while they speak, this doesn't mean they are lying. However, typically when you have an itchy nose, you use forceful or longer scratches or rubs to pacify the itch. A fleeting nose touch could be a reroute of a mouth blocking gesture.

Collar Pull: Unlike simply rubbing the collar, the collar pull is another sign commonly correlated to liars. Pulling is an indicator of high stress which may be caused by lying or being discovered in a lie. Since the activation of the sympathetic nervous system typically causes a sweat, it's likely the collar pull is to bring air to a warming area. This gesture is more prominent in men than in women. Men typically wear button up shirts with collars, and sometimes with ties –

restricting the area around the neck to a natural air flow.

Women may move their hair to allow for air on the back of their neck or may ventilate their blouse.

False Positives – the Better Liars

More often than not, a manipulator wants to seem sincere thus they mimic bodily expressions that promote openness and honesty. Obviously, the body language itself is a lie, but thankfully, since there are so many intricacies to falsifying bodily information; something is going to slip.

False positives are great to look for, especially if at some point a red flag has appeared and you're wondering if your subject has been truthful. Here are a few of the false positives to look out for:

False Openness: Just like turtles that try to hide in their shells, we hide in our invisible shells when we sense danger, or the danger of discovery. Which is why people tend to hide their palms when they are lying. People who want you to think they are telling the truth may extend their arms and open their hands to show their palms. This movement mimics openness and honesty, as we've discussed previously those trying blend in or go unnoticed, like the hunched over child, are hiding something. The good liars know that, so they open their palms to you and may even smile, depending on the topic they're lying about, as a way to disarm you.

When a person is trying to show you false openness, look for other clues or ticks. What are the eyes and mouth doing? What about their feet? As you'll learn about later, listen to the words they've chosen or the tone of their voice. Later, we'll bring together all the pieces of discovering false positives, like including diction and tone.

Forced Eye Contact: Liars and manipulators are well aware of the importance of eye contact. Typically, a person who is lying may not want to make eye contact fearing that their eyes will give them away. Adept liars will stare you down and lie to your face. A way to pick up on whether or not they are trying to stare you down to appear natural, is the amount of eye contact that they make with you.

There are two ways to determine this. Get used to watching the eyes. See what normal eye contact looks like, evaluate about how long a person will look you in the eyes and how much time they spend making eye contact with you. PsyBlog points out, thanks to some eye-tracking technologies, that the typical person will make eye contact for 30-60% of the conversation and for about 7-10 seconds at a time. Talkers look less than listeners. But someone lying to you, may stare you down for longer than normal when they're talking because they are trying to monitor your reaction to their deception.

Sudden Happiness

Sudden elation or confident actions can be displayed by a manipulator who thinks they are getting away with their lies. Just like a child partaking in their stolen cookie spoils. If you're conversation is coming to an end and there has be no interference to cause a seeming high, then it's likely that the person you're talking to has realized you don't think they are lying. Especially if after this conversation the matter would dissolve away and they would 'get away with it'. The alternative is the person has just finished lying to and having sensed acceptance from you, they feel confident they've gotten away with it. You can use this to your advantage especially if you've already realized that something seems off.

The high-toe: When a person starts feel comfortable, with a situation or another person they may place their feet closer together. These positions aren't very sturdy and obviously don't make a very good fighting (flight or fleeing) stance! If the feet are together, or crossed, or if the person is balancing on one leg, they are comfortable. A sudden change in posture may signify the manifestation of an uncomfortable situation or topic. Good liars know the importance of their feet and leg's body language.

If a person is resting on their heel with their toes facing upward, they are very happy or confident. This may happen if the subject of adversity is finally passed and the individual believes they have successfully fooled you.

The genuine smile: Liars may provide a genuine

smile after they lie if your body language suggests that you have believed their lie. Remember to check the lines in the eyes.

What Books Teach About How to Lie

If you've ever looked into books on how to master your body language or how to manipulate people, you've probably seen that they take to the thought of masking body language instead of stifling it because body language is such a naturally occurring reaction it's more difficult to stop it completely than it is to *try* to pass it off as something else. Whether or not you have read these books is irrelevant, what is important is that you know people who are trying to lie to you, have probably read these books and you need to know how they are going to try to cover up their naturally occurring body language. Just as a mother knows the behavior of her lying child, you will know the behavior of a lying acquaintance or friend.

These books focus on masking the most prominent parts signs of deceit. They tell the liar that their hands and feet are the most important limbs to hide. As we've talked about before, the feet are great signals of intention. If a person is uncomfortable and shifts their feet towards the door, they want to act on the flight instinct.

It's All in the Details

The amount of detail discussed is an important factor in a story. A bad liar may try to provide excessive detail to 'prove' they're not lying. Some liars believe that the more details they provide, the more you'll believe that it's just a recap instead of a lie. This may appear as one large bramble of 'facts' and recollections, or as seemingly random additives, with an "Oh and!"

Thus, books on lying may tell the liar to keep the details short, the less there is to lie about the less there is to be caught on and the details that are lied about should be reminiscent of the truth. This allows for better lies because the pressure of recalling and regurgitating is already based on the truth so there is less to remember and stumble over.

If a liar is especially generous with their details, it leaves room for them to accidently change their story. For instance, maybe the car was red in the first story, but blue in the second iteration. Some liars just can't keep their stories straight, if different people receive different versions of the same story, it's definitely likely, and more plausible than not, that the person is lying.

Liars who repeat the same story even to the same person may change a few details in each recollection because they couldn't remember all the details from the first time. This is a dead giveaway. So, if a detail stands out to you, make a mental note of it, check for gesticulations. Ask questions and see how the person responds. If they can't keep their details straight, how can they be telling the truth?

Rehearsal: On the other hand, some bad liars have reviewed their stories so many times that it's ingrained in to their head and is told like a recording. People who lie together and have reviewed a story may use the same wording to describe things – even though they have different speech patterns. For example, if two people are suspected of working together to steal something and have rehearsed their story before your questioning you may notice the details are oddly the same.

The first person starts recalling the story: Ted and I went to the shed to grab a rake, bags, and the riding lawn mower, but when we got there it looked like it had already been broken into. The window was busted in and some of the equipment was gone.

Some of the same phrases may be present in the second person's telling of the story such as, the order of "rake, bags, and the riding lawn mower". Other tells may be, "broken into" and "busted in.

If the second person hadn't rehearsed the story or was a better versed liar, the story may go something like this, "Me and Jake needed some equipment from the shed for our job. The window was broken, he noticed it before I did. When we opened the shed up a few things were missing." Sentence structure varies, the same details are conveyed with different words and sentences. There aren't blatantly the same idiosyncrasies.

Quick Recap:

Fight of flight: This response is possible because of the activation of the sympathetic nervous system, which produces subtle signs such as: sweating, increased heart rate, and shortness of breath. Some liars may even hold their breath.

Licking lips/ hard swallows: Licking lips is a subtle way to mouth cover. Hard swallows may occur from anxiety or nervousness due to lying.

Nervousness: Nervous energy can result in fidgeting. Fidgeting can be used as a distraction against the emotions and thoughts that arise from being nervous. Distractions are typically welcomed with liars because it allows for a change of pace and an alteration of the spotlight. You won't focus on their face because they've picked up a magazine and aren't looking at you.
-

Collar Pull: Collar pulls are a sign of stress and discomfort. Liars often use this to pacify, especially if they've started sweating and want cooler air to touch their neck.

Mouth Covering: It's a way to block the words coming out of the mouth, usually used when a speaker disagrees or doesn't believe what they are saying.

False Openness: a false display of openness is used to disarm the listener and feign honesty.

Forced Eye Contact: liars want to see if the listener has believed the webs they've weaved,

High toe: a liar who think they have been believed may suddenly become confident. The high-toe is foot where the heel is down and the toes are pointing upwards. It's a sign of confidence.

Genuine Smile: A genuine smile may cross a liar's face after they've told their lie if they think that you believe them. Look at the eyes to see if a smile is genuine, often they are relaxed and crow's feet may even form.

Chapter Five: The Facial Cues

As we've iterated before, the face is a prime place to look for clues. Whether the person is touching their face or moving their face for an expression, face value has a new meaning thanks to facial cues. You can appraise what a person is saying and whether or not you should believe them by looking at their face. You'll need to consider the context and their body language to get a full, accurate report, but the face is definitely an important piece of the puzzle.

Cues:

Fight, flight or freeze.

Some of the other expressions are going to be applicable to the face. For instance, barriers. When a person wants to hide what they are seeing, it means exactly as you would guess, they don't like what they are looking at, but it could also mean they don't like what they are hearing. A person putting their hands directly over the ears would be too counter-intuitive for it to be used as an expression, it would block their ability to hear altogether and completely expose their displeasure. So instead, a sign of audible blocking would manifest as rubbing the earlobe, or blocking on the eyes.

In the introduction, we've mentioned a person may try to cover their eyes more subtly, like rubbing their brow. People who rub their eyes or brow, or block their eyes in some way, might be feeling shame. Commonly, shame accompanies displeasure, and having to see or hear about something they are ashamed of causes an eye blocking maneuver. Bad liars may show shame at trying to lie to you.

Pacifiers.

Head Rubs: Under bouts of stress, a person may rub their forehead to pacify themselves. If you watch a classroom full of students taking an exam you will see waves of individuals rubbing their forehead. That's the stress of trying to pry their brain for information to give the right answer.

Someone who is lying may rub their forehead under the stress of trying to find the right words, or the right gesture. This is especially true if they seem uncertain about what they are saying, even more so if it's something they should know easily.

This gesture may happen in replace of rubbing the back of the neck as both displays of body language mean the same thing. Sometimes students who are taking their exam (and are worried about giving the right answer whether through guess or knowledge) may rub the back of their necks to relieve the surmounting stress.

Cheek touching: A concerned, nervous or

irritated individual may touch their cheek, or other parts of their face to pacify stress induced emotions. Well versed liars and manipulators may have taught themselves not to touch their face as much, since it's giveaway of stress or nerves. An individual may not put their hands to their face just to pacify, it may also occur if they are interested or bored with the conversation.

Typically, interest looks like the pinky to middle finger closed, and the index finger opened up along the side of the face. The thumb wont usually be visible. The other common interested gesture is an open hand against the cheek, however, this may also be a sign of boredom, depending on the expression the person has when this posture is taken.

Fingers: If one's fingers are in their mouth this is similar to blocking, and can be seen when a person is feeling stress or discomfort. When you see this gesture, it may remind you of someone biting their nails (which is a nervous habit and may be displayed during a state of higher anxiety). The fingers in the mouth gesture may also manifest during doubt, uncertainty or internal strife. The person displaying this gesture doesn't know how to move forward and is currently worried.

If you start to get onto the liar's tail and they are worried you're going to discover their lies, they may display any number of the above expressions. If they think that they've distracted you from the sensitive topic and that they've convinced you they're in the clear, you may see any number of these relief gestures. Look for them if you've changed the subject off of what raised the red flag to your improved intuition.

Puffing Cheeks: If a person pulls air into their cheeks, filling them up with air before releasing the air through pursed lips, it's likely they feel relieved like they have just barely escaped something. The air may not remain in their cheeks for long, it may be as quick as taking a deep breath in and releasing it through rounded lips right after drawing the breath in. This can also double a gesture to create relief if the stress has been building for too long. It's creates a kind of meditated exhale that forces the gesticulator to take a brief second to think.

This gesture could come before a hard question's answer, or after a person has felt they've escaped something. It may be safe to say they feel like they've escaped detection if this gesture happens in combination with the slight brow rub.

Slight Brow Rub: If a person takes one finger against their eyebrow, quickly, it could a subtle version of the commonly known gesture of wiping sweat off one's brow. This one is done as a relief gesture and as mentioned above as a combination is a sure sign of being washed with relief.

If this gesture appears alone, it may also be displayed as a way to try to force a feeling of relief during a period of high stress.

Remember, pacifying behaviors follow something distasteful, such as a question, something they're saying or that you've said. The pacifier can be used for internal or external stressors, thoughts, cognitive dissonance, or something heard or seen.
As for detecting manipulation or deceit, typically lies or mentions of the lied about topic, cause distress in the person lying. Especially if they fear the repercussions of being caught.

Micro-expressions

For the sake of being thorough, we're going to cover micro-expression if only briefly. Micro-expression can easily reveal a person's genuine emotions, even without their knowledge. More advanced liars have practiced covering up the most obvious expressions; but even these individuals cannot master the micro-expressions as they surpass the conscious choice. However, there remains one hindrance to our ability to use micro-expression to detect lies: their brevity.

Micro-expressions are just as you would assume, micro, and not because of their minute nature but because of their life-span: sometimes less than a quarter of a second. To really get an idea of just how miniscule that is, the average duration of a blink can be anywhere from a tenth to two-fifths of a second. To see it another way, that's comparatively, 0.25 seconds to 0.10-0.40 seconds. A micro-expression lasts for less time than some blinks.

Since these gesticulations can be so short lived, it's easy to miss them or to play them off a something else. Was that a half shoulder shrug? No, it must have been them moving their arm out of discomfort. The untrained eye and untrained detector, will miss almost all micro-expressions.

Common micro-expressions could be as miniscule as the seeming twitch of a shoulder, a cheek, a brow, or even a curl of the lip. People can't help but to express their deepest emotions in micro-expressions. Catching them and knowing what they are is key.

What They Are and How to Spot Them

Micro-expressions are full-faced expressions and are typically pure embodiments of an emotion, they occur on a subconscious level making them extremely useful in discovering what a person is really feeling. It could be a full frown, smile, or anger. These brief expressions die quickly before being replaced by a conscious expression of the person's choice.

A frown may show before a smile, but it's gone so fast it's practically invisible. A person may try to hide their anger, but they won't realize they flashed a scowled micro-expression before their polite laugh. The expression that comes after is hardly important, but it's usually faked. If you can spot the micro-expression before the fake smile, you know that the smile is faked without having to evaluate it as closely.

Normal people miss micro-expressions, they are over with almost instantly and typically require recorded playback to be spotted. However, it is possible to spot micro-expressions if you practice, but this isn't the kind of practice like writing the alphabet. It's like studying micro-expressions and intentionally trying to spot them unwaveringly until you can pick up on them. Though, some have picked up micro exceptionally quickly.

Thankfully though, if you don't want to put in the same practice as a trained clinician, you don't have to – you can fully analyze people without spotting micro-expressions, they are simply an extravagantly useful tool if you can spot them.

If you do want to learn to pick up on micro-expressions, you're in luck, it's actually relatively easy to do. You simply have to have pictures of different expressions, sadness, anger, contempt, happiness, etc. and flash them really quickly before covering them up. You may not be able to tell what the expression is the first few time that you try, and it may seem like an impossible task. However, after a while of flashing expressions it'll become easier and easier to pick up on them. You may even start to think that you've started flashing the pictures slower, but sure enough, you're just adapting amazingly well to picking up micro-expressions.

By Basil Foster and Joshua Moore

Practice

Let's jump into a scenario.

You're talking with a coworker; the topic of discussion is Janette another coworker who had made a fool of herself the other day. You start with the usual, "I can't believe she did that," and Marie smiles with a hand coming up to touch her cheek before she nods and agrees, "Yeah, I can't believe that she actually thought that the copier was voice activated. As if we would get something so luxurious." You both laugh but you notice that Marie is seemingly watching your laugh, as if to know when to stop. It strikes you as odd.

At this point we know that Marie is uncomfortable with the topic of conversation, but there is no real way to know why. She may simply feel like it could have been her who made such a fool of herself – that thought alone would be enough to cause a hand to cheek touch. To press the matter more, you could mention that Janette had said something angrily about someone putting a printout of voice activated instructions over the printer.

Picking up on her odd glance you do press the matter more, and she comments about whoever it was, did something completely uncalled for. She mentions that she's sympathetic for Janette, as she says this a hand comes to her face, only to stop short by her chin and move to her ear. She rubs it quickly before putting it back by her side, continues with how she would have hated for something like that to happen to her.

Noticing this added movement, you ask if she has any ideas on who might have placed the printout there. Her hand moves to touch the middle of her neck and she exhales with puffed cheeks through pursed lips. She admits that she was worried you thought it might be her, but that she could see James from IT doing it. You nod and ask why she thought she would be a suspect. She replies that you seemed very interested in the subject, her hands move out to show open palms, and she continues with she thought maybe you wanted to get information out of her.

From here, we can see that she's probably telling the truth. The open palm gesture seemed genuine, and she didn't display any further signs of discomfort except for when it seemed you may be interrogating her. The rest of her body language was genuine and only showed concern over your implied thoughts of her.

Recaps

Rubbing brow: Rubbing the brow is a sign of stress. It's common for students when taking an exam and may manifest if someone feels they are being interrogated or feel stressed to give the correct answer.

Puffing cheeks: Puffing of cheeks usually precedes the exhale through pursed lips, this is usually a physical manifestation of trying to relieve stress that is building up. It doesn't have to just be during relief, it can be used to try to gain relief.

Touching cheeks: When a person touches their face, it's usually to pacify themselves from stress, discomfort, or even nerves. Rubbing the face is practically a telltale sign of stress or discomfort as a person rubbing on their body usually is done to pacify. Though, beware that people may rub places that hurt or are sore.

Fingers in the mouth: This is a tall-tell sign that the individual is experiencing discomfort, stress, nerves, uncertainty, or doubt. It can be from a need for reassurance or worry that they are going to be caught in their deception.

Chapter Six: How Words Shape Reality

To analyze someone thoroughly, you must equip yourself with more tools than simple lie detection. Knowing when someone is lying is practically essential to navigating this world, but knowing the tricks that individuals employ to weave situations to their desires is also imperative. Simple phrases sway crowds in one direction or another, requests made in one manner or another may sway the outcome and if you're aware of these techniques you can prepare your guard against them. With manipulators being rampant, our guards *must* be higher and prepared.

Diction and Syntax

First and foremost, we'll talk diction and syntax and why they are important. Inexperienced liars may not realize the nuances of lies, leaving you with the opportunity to catch them in their deceit through their words with little to no effort. Experienced liars are all too aware of how their words will shape reality. They may choose their words so carefully or have prepared their stories so thoroughly it would be hard to spot their lie, if you weren't already aware of how they might weave these webs of deceit.

By Basil Foster and Joshua Moore

Slips of the Tongue
Sometimes slips of the tongues are just that, other times they may indicate something more. Since liars may not have had a lot of time to solidify their story before talking with you about it, they may be making up some of the details as they go along which could lead to a 'slip' of the tongue. When fabrications start to happen it's easy to get words and phrases and pronouns mixed up. Slips are less common in truthful answers than deceitful answers.

For instance, if a person has told you a story, and to clarify you've asked which direction they went and they start or respond with a contradiction then correct themselves, you may be looking at deceit.

Slips of the tongue may also occur during the alteration of the truth. Advanced liars know that lies based on truth are easier to get away with, but there is a drawback. Lies based on truth leave room for slip ups.

If a man goes to a party with a woman, when he told his wife he went with a male friend, he may 'accidently' refer to his friend as a female sometime is his story and correct himself. While people can naturally make this kind of mistake, they are more frequent when the truth is being manipulated to fit a certain tale. If this man displays more body language or facial cues to suggest his slip up wasn't just an accident, like stress or nervousness, it's likely he's trying to cover up his actions with a manipulated truth.

Pauses in speech
During conversation, pauses can be natural, especially when recalling older information, but unexpected pauses could be indicative of fabrication. The liar could also be mulling over what information to alter or omit. Take note of anything that follows on awkward or unexpected pause, it may prove advantageous to revisit the topic later on.

Pauses could also signify a chance to choose words. Commonly, a person may pause to think of the words they need to use, especially if they are trying to keep from stepping on toes. This same principle is applied to what word choice would create the least resistance in their prey if they are a manipulator. Pausing in words may remind you of the primitive body language freezing. It's true that pausing in speech could directly correlate because it allows the brain time to analyze what it should do next.

Speech Patterns and Pace
The same may apply to a change in a person's speech pattern or pace. Take note of how fast the person talks, how often they pause and the general pace and pattern. If there are changes to this pace, a slow speaker suddenly forces words out in a frenzy, or a quick talker starts to slow down, or even those who pause a lot stop pauses, or vice versa, take note. Changes in speech usually happen to allow the mind to adjust. Whether it is figuring out what to say next or trying to get words out before their oddity is

noticed, the difference is a sign.

Always watch the person who is speaking, whether you are evaluation their body language or facial cues, if moments where speech patterns or pace start to change also correlate with changes in their body language (from relaxed to stressed) then take note of what they're saying, be sure to come back to it and pry into it more.

Miscellaneous Oddities

When emotions aren't obviously high and the person suddenly changes their pitch or their voice wavers, it's likely they are worried or nervous. Individuals take on a higher pitch during stressful moments. A person's voice may waver if they are nervous or uncertain. It's important to note that if the person you're talking to feels like you are interrogating them, you yourself may be causing them stress. It may also occur if the person is worried that their honesty may be mistaken for deceit or misinterpreted, this especially true if you've made them feel like they should be worried.

If you make it obvious that you're searching for answers or looking for lies, you will undoubtedly cause stress in whoever you are talking to. So be aware of how you're acting and speaking.

Consider the fact that someone who is lying may suddenly take a more formal tone. People under stress start to lose slang and speak more deliberately. Thus, liars tend to speak out contractions, instead of saying, "I didn't do it" they may choose to say, "I did not do it" to allow for an emphasis on the word, "not".

Which brings us to another common cue to look out for: be oddly enunciated words. Typically, the word no or other negatives are used and oddly enunciated to show someone did or didn't take an action.

Here are a few things to look for when someone is saying no, especially if they've started to enunciate the world strangely.

- Hesitation. Hesitation before an affirmative or negative could be the split-second needed to decide to lie or not. While there is a chance they may have chosen not to lie, take note of the topic that they've been hesitant on responding.
- Your subject looks in another direction. For example, if they were making eye contact with you and then suddenly look away while speaking their negative or affirmative.
- Close their eyes for extended periods of time. If they close their eyes they could be blocking the image of you as they lie.

Practice

This far into the book, you should be pretty adept at observing others and picking up on their body language, but now it's time to train your ears. If you have a hard time multitasking, try getting used to listening for the previous mentioned things: slips of the tongue, pauses in speech, or changes to speech pace or patterns. Make a mental note of what's being said. Continue this exercise until you've gotten listening down pat. It may take a few days to adjust, likely as long as it too you to adjust to observing people and looking for specific signs.

Once you've become more accustomed to listening, try paying attention to when their body language and speech preform a combination of stress displays. Thankfully, these things can be practiced throughout the day with little need to take time out of your day. Unless you're a big introvert, you probably have conversations pretty regularly to pay attention to.

How Requests are Made

Through years of research, we've concluded there are good ways to ask for things and bad ways to ask for things. Good manipulators know the difference.

Foot in the Door Phenomenon

This technique may sound familiar. Salesmen tend to put their foot in the door in order to offer product information when a door is closing in their face. Have you ever wondered why? Reopening the door is the first step to getting the buyer to purchase an in-home product. If the salesman's victim is willing enough to reopen the door, what then is keeping them from also complying with buying a product? Salesman know if they start with a request and it is accepted (being listened to instead of closing the door completely), but there is left room for another request (the crack in the door) then a person is more likely to accept a second large request (buying a product) if it is preceded by a smaller, accepted request (allowing the salesperson to put their foot in the door).

Putting our foot in the door, would be like asking a friend to borrow twenty dollars, before asking the same friend to also run a marathon for charity. Over half of people who are asked to comply to a small request and whom accepted, complied to the second, larger request. This gives merit to the saying "Give him an inch and he'll take a mile", we have to admit there was wisdom in some of the older sayings. Though we may not have understood why this concept worked when the phrase was originally coined, we can do well to explain it now (hint: one aspect is that the first requests' acceptance primes for an altruistic response again).

Foot in the Door Phenomenon works because once a person has agreed to the first request, the one subjected to the request feels more involved, there is now a commitment (even if it's a small one). Commitment is another major factor when considering manipulation. How often do you buy the same brand's product because it's what you're used to, or because they have come out with something better? With that commitment made, the one subjected to the request feels obliged to accept the next request. Sure, you'll upgrade models with the same company, even though there is only one advantage to the new product (and even though your current model works perfectly fine).

Low-Balling
Surprisingly enough, this next technique is practically the complete opposite of the first one. To continue our first setting, we'll still talk about salesmen, but we'll move to another well-known incident, the car salesmen, (it's not really surprising to consider what they do as manipulation). To be more precise, it is what they do with the price that is manipulation. Low-Balling is the technique of offering a product at one price and then raising it. This can be done with cars or any product or request, really. It's the very process of inflation in economy or maximizing profit by seeing what the highest price a customer will buy a product for is. Either way, for companies this is their favorite manipulation technique, but companies aren't the only ones using this technique.

A car salesman will offer a car at one price, a whopping twenty-two thousand dollars for the brand-new car. Then after the customer accepts to pay for the car at this price, there are suddenly some drawbacks in some of the unseen paperwork, in which the salesmen 'regretfully' (yeah right) informs the customer that the price is no longer twenty-two thousand dollars but twenty-four thousand (but hey, you get that cool looking spoiler and some added volume to the stereo). Or, the model that you wanted specifically wasn't in stock, so they had to upgrade you, but they'll give you a discount (one that still leaves the price higher than it originally was), but you can have the cool accessories. Since the customer or prey, has already agreed to the first price, it isn't difficult to get them to budge and accept the second, even higher price too.

This doesn't just apply to salesmen though. Your spouse, friend or coworker may ask you to do something small that you don't really want to do (especially true if they know that you may have a hard time saying no), it may just be a small inconvenience but your acceptance signals a readiness to comply to a larger request. So, once you've accepted they may add, "Oh, and while you're add it..." this is a common technique employed by numerous individuals. While say may innocently and ignorantly use this technique (only asking in this manner because it has worked before), others are using it solely because it's a proven method of manipulation.

Knowing about these psychological inclinations can help you abstain from falling into the traps. If you have a hard time saying no and don't mind helping with the first small task but really don't want to do the second larger task, remind yourself why you feel inclined to do the second and that you don't have to. Use this time to practice saying no.

By Basil Foster and Joshua Moore

It may behoove you to practice noticing this technique's usage. Try to evaluate requests and see if they are done through foot in the door or by low balling. If you notice that they are, practice saying no. The easier you can identify these situations the easier it will be to notice when they are used malevolently as a method of manipulation.

Chapter Seven: Analyzing Matters of the Heart/Home

Reading into the matters of the heart is tricky business. Even people you love have reasons for withholding information or seemingly spinning the truth. Imagine how hard it would be for your significant other to plan surprises for you if you knew every single time they were hiding something.
On the matter of hidden intentions, even when devoted to others, individuals may still want some semblance of privacy. Having privacy does not equate to devious behaviors. So, before you start to delve into reading the matters of the heart, try to remember trust is essential. Tread through this chapter lightly.

Whether you've just started dating your significant other or you've been together for a while, chances are you know their baseline behavior. All incongruences should be compared to their baseline. If you're going to use this section to determine whether or not someone is interested in you, it's advisable to pick up on their personality type and establish a baseline. – *Individuals who are nervous and trying to impress another may exhibit more nervous tendencies making it arduous to determine a baseline.*

By Basil Foster and Joshua Moore

Lying and Cheating

The sad truth is that sometimes significant others lie. Lies aren't always indicative of earth-shattering news. In relationships, fear could be a prime motivator for deceit. For instance, your significant other (SO), could be afraid to disappoint you, afraid of what you'll think of them, afraid they haven't made enough profess for you, or are worried you won't react well to any number of things. Lies may even manifest because you SO hasn't come to terms with something on their own.

Regardless of the reasons, or what lying may indicate, you'll want to know why your SO is being deceitful. Naturally, you may fear the worst.

You may notice a change in their behavior, or stories that just aren't adding up. If that's the case, it's time to start monitoring their facial expressions, body language, and words. Just because they are intimate with you doesn't mean they won't express some of the same tells that you've learned in prior chapters. Keep in mind the same tips, one gesticulation is just not enough evidence.

Inconsistencies

Chances are, you know your SO, you may even know them so well they could be an extension of yourself. This prior information is crucial. Inconsistencies in their day to day life, their emotions, their behaviors, are all cues that more is brewing below the surface than they are letting on.

Distance is a telltale sign that your SO may be weavings webs. When people that are usually really intimate start to allow distance to separate them, whether physical, mental or emotional it's a sign that something is going on. For example, if you after work your SO comes home and usually requires twenty minutes to themselves but instead, they take hours where they don't want to talk or be close to you – that's an obvious tell something is amiss. Signs may not always be this obvious but when they are, try not to shrug them off.

Discomfort: If you're with someone, regardless of if it is just dating or something more and your SO shows a level of discomfort around you, or around certain topics that aren't taboo, they may feel awkward trying to hide, hold secrets or even lying to you. Typically, the reason you're dating someone is because you both feel comfortable around each other. Unexplained discomfort is usually a sign that something more is going, and noticing when it occurs will alert you to what may be going on below the surface.

If, they only act uncomfortable with you when you mention, loyalty, or love (and love has already been introduced to your relationship and this isn't a first-time mention) you may want to consider the possibility of infidelity within the relationship or a waning of their emotions towards you. – That isn't to say that at the first sign of discomfort in your relationship you should abandon ship, but you should definitely start investigating subtly and try talking to your partner about what is bothering them.

When you start your conversation be on the lookout for uncommon or unusual expressions for them, for facial cues or body language that may suggest deceit. Finding out your answers could be the same as if you were talking to anyone else. They may still touch their face, their collarbone or pull on the collar of their shirt, or any other expression we discussed in the previous chapters.

Awkward Expressions: Chances are you know how your significant other reactions and acts in certain situations. When they smile and how they smile. If you notice that their expressions seemed forced or are awkward, it may be because they aren't as genuine as usual.

Defensive: Another usually blatant sign of manipulation or deceit would be a very defensive SO. Without contrition there is no defensive SO, especially if being defensive isn't usually within their nature.

Unresponsive: Communication has always been key in relationships, a sudden change in how your SO responds to you or if they stop responding altogether, then find out why. Anger is the primary reason to stop communication within a relationship but if your SO just doesn't want to let on to their deceit or discontentment, they may be defensive and unresponsive to questions you ask that would normally

Matters of the Home

When considering matters of your home, there could be more members than just you and your SO. If the two of you have children, other family staying or just roommates, all of these individuals may try to pull some sort of wool over your eyes while they're there.

Your roommate may try to cover up their supposed *borrowing* of your money, clothes, items or other things. Children may try to get away with breaking the rules and other family members may just try to move about with their own prerogative, regardless of what that is. In situations like these you're at a disadvantage if you can't spot their manipulative behavior and lying cues.

Confrontation

Confrontation of the transgressor can be a tricky situation. As you will learn about in the next chapter, those who have lied don't want to admit that they are wrong and may already have trouble owning up to their own shortcomings. These insecurities can create a backlash against you, if you question the transgressor's motive and intentions or try to expose them.

If the person you have caught by surmounting evidence of if you've nabbed them red-handed, then you have to be conscientious of the possibility of an angry response. Those who don't want to be exposed can go to great, even unreasonable lengths to cover up their secrets, as we'll expound upon later, this is essentially how a spouse starts gaslighting.

Being lied to will ruffle anyone's feathers, but don't let it get under your skin when you're approaching the subject. Starting your conversation out angrily will only escalate the matter. So, don't attack your spouse, or anyone in your home, verbally, mentally or emotionally. Approach them openly and benevolently. Try to remain open-minded and ready to understand why they have done what they have done – especially if this is your SO.

In loving, healthy relationships you may find your spouse only lies when they fear disappointing you. If you've taken a loving approach to confronting them about their lie then you may realize how you can help them feel better about these things and prevent the lies from happening in the future.

In the same breath though, there are chronic liars. These are the ones who you can't just forgive and move on in the relationship with as over time the trust the relationship was built on will deteriorate. Simply said, a chronic liar will always have to fight their impulse to lie and you will almost always find yourself on guard about the things they tell you. If you do find a chronic liar in your life, whether your SO, a person in your family or a child, get to know their specific tells, as they may be different from some of the things we've discussed. As you know, they have experience lying and have tried to master the art of getting away with it.

Gaslighting

If you're not familiar with this term, don't worry. Gaslighting is the process of convincing someone that they are crazy, it uses a convoluted combination of manipulation factor to create a desired end result. Gaslighting requires a gaslighter (those who employ this technique of manipulation) to systematically discredit the prey; to do this the gaslighter must first make the prey feel like they themselves may be unstable. This usually spurns from an abuser who wants to make sure their victim cannot seek refuge and won't be believed by friends and family if they ever come forward as having been abused.

This was seen frequently in the times were females were forced to be dependent upon their husbands. Certain husbands wanted to discredit their wives for various reasons and there was no better way to do it than to make everyone, including the wife think that she was crazy. A sad and unfortunate reality. An even more melancholy truth is that this manipulation technique is still used today.

Have you ever been told you're crazy? Chances are you have, but has anyone ever tried and dedicated themselves to convincing you that you were indeed crazy? We find that gaslighters go to insane lengths to convince their victims. In the

By Basil Foster and Joshua Moore

famous 1944 movie "Gaslight" the husband would do various things, like turning on the lights and then tell his wife that she did it. Of course, because she didn't do those things she had no memory of them, in which case he insisted she did and that she just didn't remember. It's always heartbreaking when someone you love takes advantage of your trust and insists that you're crazy to the point that you believe them. While you may only find dedicated gaslighters to be those who are of the manipulator type or are a sociopath, you as one who has worked to defend against liars and manipulators have to be aware of this occurrence.

Gaslighting don't just tell the prey that they crazy and systematically convince them of it, they will start to tell others that the prey is starting to go crazy. This creates a situation where the friends and family members are concerned, and those friends also try to convince the prey that he/she is crazy or needs help, but it's okay because they want to offer support. These friends and family members are genuinely concerned and have taken the manipulator at face value, they are going to do all that they can to also convince the prey to face the 'reality' of their disorder. This will go on and on, and only get worse as it continues until the prey starts to accept that fact that maybe, they are truly crazy and that's why they don't remember things or that's why strange things are happening. With what seems to be an army against you, there is hardly any way to cling to the real world of what you once knew. The longer this goes on, the further into victory the gaslighter goes, and the further into dread and despair and sadly, acceptance the prey goes.

Be aware that there are people out there who want nothing more than to take advantage of the weak and convince them they're the crazy ones. Use the tips and tricks in this book to identify these individuals and stay clear away from them. Protect your friends and family from them.
If you confront someone about their lies and they try to turn it onto you, they may have gaslighter tendencies. If they are willing to go to seemingly unreasonable lengths; solid advice to take would be to stay away from them.

Chapter Eight: Catching the Tiger by the Tail

Be mindful of your environment and other factors that may cause a shift in your subject's behavior. Always find other confirmations when you think you've discovered someone has delved into the world of deceit. If not, you may be making a fool of yourself and discrediting a perfectly honest individual.

What Do the Professionals Do?

Professionals have likely studied body language for years before finally using it on their job. With a mixture of talent and education, astute observing quickly bag the liars and frees the innocent; but how can you as an average individual definitively know that someone is lying? Employ some of the very same techniques, that's how!

Take a moment to imagine that you're an interrogator and you're to go to a woman's house, it's believed that she has been hiding her fugitive son in her home. This is a regular citizen, you can't very well shine the lights in her eyes, slam your hands down on a table while flaunting your authoritative stance and demand answers. That provides a bad public image.

Instead you and your partner ask her questions.

If she's nice she's invited you in, if not you're standing at her doorstep. When you start your inquiries, you watch her eyes, her arms her hands. For the most part, she is calm and collected. On occasion she scratches her neck area and her eyes have shifted a few times. She's shifted her weight. You've already asked if her son is in the home, she's answered no, during this answer she didn't display any stress related gesticulations. You're about to wrap all of this up, but you decide to ask one more question, "Is it possible that your son is on the premise, without your knowledge?" she brings her hand up to her neck, not to scratch but only for a moment before dropping it.

That signal there is just a clue. That alone is not enough to get a search warrant. Instead, the interrogator now knows that it's possible the son has 'snuck' onto the premise when the woman was not around. She may be aware of his presence, but she had not harbored him. Knowing this, you can act like you're ready to leave, but before letting her close the door, tell her you just want to clarify your records. You ask her several of your questions again, not just the ones about if her son is in the home. This time, though, you reword the ones related to her knowledge of the son's whereabouts and if he is in the home. If she displays signs of discomfort at these questions again, you can start to pry. Find the right way to word the question to get the affirmative.

One gesticulation is a hint. Reoccurring

gesticulations can point you in the right direction. They are not answers and cannot be counted an answer. Use them to find the answer, like a detective on a case, an interrogator getting an answer, or a spy mounting evidence.

Backwards
Police officers ask individuals to say the alphabet backwards to find out if they are intoxicated. If you've never tried to say the alphabet backwards, chances are you'll find it quite difficult. The mental ability to reverse the alphabet is dependent upon sobriety because you'll have to be able to spend time reasoning. Knowing the alphabet allows you to work your way towards your answer.

You can ask for a story backwards to find out if a person is lying. If you've told a story you remember, chances are you can reason your way through telling it backwards. There may be a few questionable areas, but with some time you could do it. If you try telling a story you don't know backwards, you're probably not going to be able to piece the details together correctly. If you want to do this subtly, try asking for what happened before a point in the story, as if you have forgotten or are trying to piece it together yourself. If you act like you're figuring out the timeline, someone telling the truth should have no problem filling in the gaps.

Beware of distractions. Liars know that if they distract their interrogator they can run down a different rabbit hole. Women may flash a man, men may compliment the woman. These ploys are moves to alter the spotlight of the conversation. Without the light, the lies are left in the dark.

If All Else Fails:
Some people would rather rip off one of their own limbs than admit that they are wrong. Now, if that very same personality has lied to you and you have confronted them about that lie, do you imagine that they would just admit they were wrong and lied to cover their own ego? Not likely. Manipulators, sociopaths, and gaslighters would all fight tooth and nail to 'prove' their lives were 'true'. Only those who have really become comfortable with themselves and failure are okay admitting to their own mistakes.

Lies are already being told to save face, admitting to that lie would destroy all attempts that the person has made at saving face. So, while some people may never, even in the face of surmounting evidence admit that they have lied or that they are wrong, you will be able to weasel the truth out of some less determined individuals. You'll have to learn when to accept that someone just won't admit their lie, that doesn't mean they haven't lied, especially if you've gotten all the evidence pointing to the contrary, but getting angry or upset with them will get you nowhere.

Some people have convinced themselves of their own lies so thoroughly that when you are confronting them with the truth they would feel like you're personally attacking them. No one likes being attacked personally, and doing so usually creates massive backlash. Be aware of this possibility. Professionals face it all the time, an officer may have to arrest a man that has DNA evidence against him while he yells that he's innocent. While innocents have been incarcerated, real criminals yell their lies of innocence until they can't speak anymore. If professionals can't get a truly guilty person to admit their guilt, you may never get some individuals to admit their lies.

Now, as we talked about in the matters of heart and home chapter, always confront people with kindness and openness. People are too aggressive when they feel they are being challenged for you to throw caution to the wind.

Thankfully, some individuals when caught in their deceit will just admit that they lied and own up to it. Manipulators on the other hand, won't be so privy to admitting they were just a manipulator from the beginning, they just may phase themselves out of your life.

Try It

A great saying goes, "if you can't beat them, join them." While we haven't picked a fight with a manipulator, we do want to uncover how they think. After all, knowing your enemy is the first step in warfare.

Get to know the nitty gritty of lying. Do you know what signs you display when you try to lie? What happens when you think about lying, talking about it, or are in the act of lying? Watch yourself in the mirror as you formulate webs of deceit. Practice lying in the mirror. Think about what would happen if your lie was discovered. Watch for your cues. What gesticulations do you display? How do you react? Chances are, you aren't the only one. You've likely even noticed a few of the things we've talked about. Get to know these hints intimately.

We don't suggest actually lying to others, for the same reason you don't want others to lie to you. Just simply get an understanding for what is like to be in the liar's skin.

Here is Some Practice:

To help make sure you can pick up on what the different displays of body language/facial cues/voice cues mean, try your hand at the below scenario.

You've realized that your significant other has been acting strangely lately. Now, he doesn't answer your calls promptly, he will delay answering your questions and is often off doing things and spinning stories that don't seem to add up.

Finally, after fretting about it until you were practically sick, you ask him about it. At first, he seems to blow off your question and tries to change the subject, but relentlessly you prod forward. Finally, he seems willing to communicate.

To start, you point out that he has been acting strangely lately. With puffed out cheeks he responds that work has just been changing schedules and tasks on him lately, and it has him a bit frazzled. He makes a normal amount of eye contact with you and grabs your hands in his as he speaks.

With a sigh, you tell him that you feel he is falling out of love with you. "What?" is his response, his voice seemed to be a higher pitch. His eyes widened for a moment. Then he rubs the back of his neck and breaks eye contact with you. You continue forward by asking him if he is hiding something from you. He hesitates to respond; his movements cease momentarily before he looks back up at you and leans closer as he tells you he loves you.

From the current state of the conversation what conclusions have you drawn? Is he just stressed from work and carrying it over inadvertently? Is he cheating? Is he lying, if so what aspect of the conversation points to a lie? Do you feel like he is hiding something?

You don't take the distraction bait and instead ask again if he is hiding something. He looks you and rubs his forehead. There is no response, so you ask if he is cheating on you. His response is quick, and he looks at you as he says, "No. I'm not cheating on you." He lays his hand open as he answers, "I would never cheat on you."

Take some time to process this scenario. When you're ready read the next paragraph to see what was going on.

At first, your SO's cheeks blow out air to relieve the stress of having to lie to you, he's being open with you because he feels his lie is justified and necessary. He makes contact with you to show that he's still on your side. He's shocked when you tell you feel like he has fallen out of love with you, because it couldn't be further from the truth, he's unsure what he should do next and rubs his neck to relieve the stress of his earlier lie causing you such worry. He looks away because of remorse.

He hesitates to respond to if he is hiding something from you because yes, he is hiding something from you, but not for the reason you think. He tries to reassure you with his love to show that his love is not waning and there is nothing to worry about. His answer to if he is cheating on you is sincere, his open palm is a sign of being open and honest with you.

But inevitably you're missing information: Your significant other has been trying to plan the right way to ask you to marry him. He's been visiting jewelers and asking his friends for advice. He's been trying to plan the right way to ask you. So, while yes, he was hiding information from you, it was by no means something horrible.

The above scenario is done to illustrate how if you want to find a liar, you will find a liar, but if you cannot piece together multiple pieces of the puzzle then you can come to the wrong conclusion very easily, especially if you're missing information. It's easy to miss information, especially if you don't know it's there. You can't be expected to know something you don't know.

When trying to read people, it's important to gather as much information as possible to get the biggest picture possible. You'll want to keep an open mind because even after as thorough research and observation as possible, you may still be missing information. It's always a possibility. If you feel like you may not have a full picture, try micro conversations that give you bits of information or leads that you can follow to more information. For instance, had you started your conversation with your SO by voicing your doubts and asking him to be open with you, you may have been able to glean enough information to realize that he had something planned and was hiding that from you, but that he loved you and definitely wasn't doing anything devious. If you still didn't believe him, you could at least use that information to learn more about the situation. Hopefully though at some point you realized that you trusted him enough and that you'd find out eventually.

Great detectives, great analyzers and great people-readers stick to more concrete aspects.

They realize that a stress indicator could be for any reason and thus if they want to use it as evidence feel obliged to further rule out of possibilities.
Now with your tools, knowledge and wisdom you are about to become a great people reader.

By Basil Foster and Joshua Moore

FREE DOWNLOAD

INSIGHTFUL GROWTH STRATEGIES FOR YOUR PERSONAL AND PROFESSIONAL SUCCESS!

Sign up here to get a free copy of The Growth Mindset book and more:
www.frenchnumber.net/growth

You may also like...
EMOTIONAL INTELLIGENCE SPECTRUM
EXPLORE YOUR EMOTIONS AND IMPROVE YOUR
INTRAPERSONAL INTELLIGENCE
BY JOSHUA MOORE AND HELEN GLASGOW

By Basil Foster and Joshua Moore

Emotional Intelligence Spectrum is the one book you need to buy if you've been curious about Emotional Intelligence, how it affects you personally, how to interpret EI in others and how to utilize Emotional Quotient in every aspect of your life.

Once you understand how EQ works, by taking a simple test, which is included in this guide, you will learn to harness the power of Emotional Intelligence and use it to further your career as you learn how to connect with people better.

You may also like...
I AM AN EMPATH
ENERGY HEALING GUIDE FOR EMPATHIC AND
HIGHLY SENSITIVE PEOPLE
BY JOSHUA MOORE

By Basil Foster and Joshua Moore

Am an Empath is an empathy guide on managing emotional anxiety, coping with being over emotional and using intuition to benefit from this sensitivity in your everyday life – the problems highly sensitive people normally face.

Through recongnizing how to control emotions you have the potential to make the most of being in tune with your emotions and understanding the feelings of people around you.
Begin your journey to a fulfilling life of awareness and support today!

You may also like...
MAKE ROOM FOR MINIMALISM
A PRACTICAL GUIDE TO SIMPLE AND
SUSTAINABLE LIVING
BY JOSHUA MOORE

By Basil Foster and Joshua Moore

Make Room for Minimalism is a clear cut yet powerful, step-by-step introduction to minimalism, a sustainable lifestyle that will enable you to finally clear away all the physical, mental and spiritual clutter that fills many of our current stress filled lives. Minimalism will help you redefine what is truly meaningful in your life.

Eager to experience the world of minimalism? Add a single copy of **Make Room for Minimalism** to your library now, and start counting the books you will no longer need!

FNº

Presented by French Number Publishing
French Number Publishing is an independent publishing house headquartered in Paris, France with offices in North America, Europe, and Asia. FNº is committed to connect the most promising writers to readers from all around the world. Together we aim to explore the most challenging issues on a large variety of topics that are of interest to the modern society.

FNº

By Basil Foster and Joshua Moore

All rights Reserved. No part of this publication or the information in it may be quoted from or reproduced in any form by means such as printing, scanning, photocopying or otherwise without prior written permission of the copyright holder.

Disclaimer and Terms of Use: Effort has been made to ensure that the information in this book is accurate and complete, however, the author and the publisher do not warrant the accuracy of the information, text and graphics contained within the book due to the rapidly changing nature of science, research, known and unknown facts and internet. The Author and the publisher do not hold any responsibility for errors, omissions or contrary interpretation of the subject matter herein. This book is presented solely for motivational and informational purposes only.

Made in the USA
Las Vegas, NV
05 April 2025